Sri Sathya Sai Baba coloring

Volume 7

Sri Sathya Sai Baba
was a spiritual master
famous Indian, an Avatar.

An Avatar is a divine incarnation
that originates in a human body
who possesses the faculties of omnipotence
omnipresence and omniscience.

All spiritual and divine qualities are incarnated to perfection in Sai Baba:
Purity, Love, Truth,
Peace, Right Action, Non-Violence.

He is a divine master, as were Buddha, Krishna or Jesus Christ.

rust in Me and
our prayer shall
be answered

Sathya Sai Baba is the incarnation
the most powerful of God
never come to earth,
and there will be no others at His level
in the next sixty centuries.

He taught how to walk the path
from Perfection, to the knowledge of God,
to the realization of the purpose of our lives.

Sai Baba is the Father who sent Jesus
and we are also God,
but we have forgotten it.

" I am neither Guru nor God.
I am you; You are I;
This is the truth.
There is no distinction.
The apparent differences
are the illusion.
You are waves; I am the ocean.
Know that and be free, be Divine. "

CHILDREN OF IMMORTALITY

Immortality children!
Remember that you are created
In my image and likeness.
Perfect!

Comply with this picture,
In all occasions, at all levels.
Live like Masters!
Walk in this world
with your head up,
Your planing spirits ...
Your hearts open to Love ...
And believe in yourself
and God in you.
Then everything will be fine.

The earth is only
a manifestation of my Being,
Made of my life!

Wherever you look, I am here.
Wherever you walk, I am here.
Whoever you contact, I am that person.
I am in everyone, in all My splendor.

See me everywhere,
Talk to Me and love Me,
Who am in everyone.

So of everyone, I will answer
And you will lead to Glory.
You can not see me
in one place without seeing me elsewhere
Because I fill all the space.

*You can not escape.
Or do anything in secret,
Because there are no secrets with Me.*

*Live ... Live ... Live ...
in perfect harmony
With My Laws, and
wonders will follow.*

*Think now.
Mistakes would prevent free flow
From the Essence of
My Being through you?
Ask me right now
to reveal your mistakes
In the silence of your meditation.*

*Let the old memories
come back to you,
Since My subsonscient in you ...
Old patterns ...
Old feelings and forgotten thoughts.*

*Now immerse them
in the Ocean of Light,
Dissolve them in the consciousness
So that you can be
real emblems of My Being.*

*Right now,
Visualize my burning flame
Rising higher and higher
As she burns through you.*

*It's a flame that refreshes,
Cleans and heals,*

*Which softens the buried sadness ...
And leave you calm and quiet.*

*Rest in My Love.
Leave everything you experienced.*

*During your many lives
until today, melt and dissolve
in My comforting Light.*

*Children of My Being!
Come dissolve in Me
your sorrows and your fears.
Let me erase
All your karmas.*

*Return to My Consciousness, which is
Your own true Consciousness.*

*Leave your poor identity
human disappear right now,
while you come to Me,
Who embodies your Inner Self.*

*You are now
My radiant and glorious self ...
Henceforth not separated from Me.
Melted in Me ... Merged with Me ...
Join me!*

Sathya Sai Baba

Découvrir également :
Ganesh

Krishna

Bouddha

Shiva

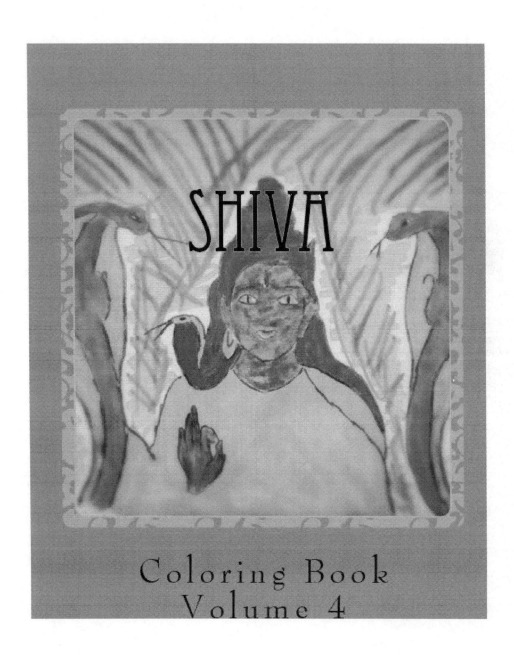

Tara

A gift for you

Hi Keshava, Enjoy your gift! From HARI H SUDAN

amazon Gift Receipt

Send a Thank You Note
You can learn more about your gift or start a return here too.

Scan using the Amazon app or visit
http://a.co/bPNXGJE

Sri Sathya Sai Baba coloring
Order ID: 114-6615809-0667449   Ordered on September 1, 2018

Made in the USA
Lexington, KY
01 September 2018